Selected and New Poems
1980—1997

Also by Lotte Kramer

Ice Break
(Annakinn, 1980)

Family Arrivals
(Poet and Printer, 1981 & 1992)

A Lifelong House
(Hippopotamus Press, 1983)

The Shoemaker's Wife
(Hippopotamus Press, 1987)

Earthquake and other poems
(Rockingham Press, 1994)

The Desecration of Trees
(Hippopotamus Press, 1994)

Lotte Kramer

Selected and New Poems 1980–1997

Rockingham Press

in association with the European Jewish Publication Society

Published in 1997
by
The Rockingham Press
11 Musley Lane,
Ware, Herts
SG12 7EN

British Library Cataloguing-in-Publication Data

A catalogue record for this book
is available from the British Library

ISBN 1 873468 53 9

Printed in Great Britain
by Biddles Limited, Guildford

Printed on Recycled Paper

The European Jewish Publication Society is a registered
charity which gives grants to assist in the publication and
distribution of books relevant to Jewish literature, history,
religion, philosophy, politics and culture. EJPS c/o The
Joseph Levy Charitable Foundation, 37-43 Sackville Street,
London W1X 2DL

For Joanna and Robert

Acknowledgements

Acknowledgements are due to the editors of the following publications in which some of the new poems first appeared: *Acumen, Agenda, Ambit, European Judaism, The Interpreter's House, New Statesman, Other Poetry, The Spectator, Spokes* and *Stand.* Acknowledgement is also due to Michael Zylberberg for the story (published in *Jewish Festivals*, edited by H. Schauff) which I have used in the poem "Warsaw Vigil".

For the selected poems, I have to thank the publishers of my individual collections: Annakin for *Ice-Break*, Poet and Printer for *Family Arrivals*, Hippopotamus Press for *A Lifelong House, The Shoemaker's Wife* and *The Desecration of Trees*, and Rockingham Press for *Earthquake and other poems*.

Contents

From THE SHOEMAKER'S WIFE (1987)

From EARTHQUAKE AND OTHER POEMS (1994)

From THE DESECRATION OF TREES (1994)

From
ICE-BREAK (1980)

ICE-BREAK

Snow and ice have lain
Rich and fat on the grass
For days,
On river and lake the silver
Is sitting as stubborn
As oil,
Each blade and twig has a
Metal skin of its own.

The light cuts right through the years
And I find myself small
By the side
Of my father, quite close to his hand,
Our feet step in careful tread on the ice,
The Rhine
Now a new white street without end,
The reliable river vanished or dead.

Yet alive
With a fun-fair crowd
On its broad, hard chest,
As men
Use the solid water instead of earth
And dancing deny its escape
And birth,
But the poem insists on its flow
With the ice-break of words.

FINAL SOLUTION

The've been mowing down the wild grasses,
And the camomile in the lane
Is buried under black tarmac;
Its scent used to rise to my brain
And remind me of tea that my mother
Was brewing to soothe away pain.

And they, who were cutting the grasses
And stifling the weed in the lane,
Did they care for the shape of a flower,
Did they know of the herb for the pain?

And they, who had ordered the killing
On well-polished telephones —
Was it easy when men are so willing
To diminish each other like stones?

HOMECOMING

Each coming home hides tears behind the smile;
A splintered sun defers the losing day
Till night returns in island skeletons.

Too much perfection claims a stubborn prize;
And like a mole, I tunnel back my way
To pile some earth on joy's great marathon.

I have to take up mending for a while,
And stitch a patchwork cover, where I stay,
To mask the weeping sores of Babylon.

I know, I'll never reach that careless climb,
Or walk through someone until white grows grey:
I travel with my luggage bone to bone.

ASPECTS OF HOME

Home is this field,
This quietness
That confiscates all else.
Here shadows mark
Solidity —
Machinery content
To know its route —
As though our feet
Could tread this earth for ever.
To lose this clay
Would blind me, lock
The sky into the night.
But mostly home
Is where we meet:
In unseen countryside
From chance to word —
And filter thoughts
We never hoped to enter.

EASTER WEEKEND

On the first day
Nothing but clouds coffined the sky
Hooding new grass and Yorkshire stone.
Wind stole our breath and tightened our skin;
The old town ached in buckled houses.

On the second day
We searched the monks' path in the arched abbey,
Where water doubled a crumbling message
And rivalled a chant, older than felled trees:
Their timber blood-red, their still years exposed.

On the third day
As the moor's ground met our feet in sprung heather,
The protesting croak of a nesting bird
Shattered a grey cloud — and the blue light struck
Each coarse-coiled scrub — like a duel of limbs.

IF

If it were a beginning
I would mourn the lateness,

If love were mother-tongue between us
It could become a religion,

If yesterday's despair
Had its root in all presences,

Then — the God of trees
Would raise us both

From a sapling's paradise
To the gate of always.

A SEPARATE STARE

For days I wondered whom I met,
    Then, in that dream:
A face, dated and near, the lips
    A scarlet line,
And eyes as large and quizzical
    As question marks.

So many dreams are lost when we
    Awake and fall;
But not this one: that separate stare.
    Who can she be —
Who is the I she clearly saw —
    If we find truth
In dreams, what right and absolute
    Can she command?

I search for faces I have known
    In rooms and lanes,
I look for warning corners where
    She might have stood,
I let her strangeness free me from
    My mirrored self.

JOY

When you point at a house or a church
For me to look at as we pass,
I want to shout: "Yes, yes,
That's how we collect stars
Here, on earth, with two pairs of eyes!"

When you show me a leaf or a flower
Distilling their antique history
In a few cut-glass words —
They scrape my rind of joy
To moments of permanent order.

NINE HERONS ON
RECLAIMED LAND

Nine herons on a dark-ploughed field
Surprised by sun
That reddened through the morning frost.
They stand as carved
And motionless as this blue air.
Land falls from us
In long, stiff tongues that grip the sky.
It is not strange
That on this nameless face of earth
One stands apart —
The ninth, the odd, the single one:
Here every breath
Is ominous of waiting sea ...

IN A COMMON ROOM

Today the mist
Sweats on the window-sill,
And, unresolved as we,
It seems to slide across the afternoon.

We sip our tea
And talk of things, of pain
Outside ourselves,
Hiding the drift and debris in our bones.

Behind us,
In a room, so many autumn-lives
Stitch words to clothes,
And find some solace in a garment's touch,

While we
Choose words, and empty hands,
And moody fingers
That can bless and abdicate on paper.

KNOW ME

For you
I was a glass of wine.
Maybe
The bouquet lingers,
But the glass
Broke long ago.

Look,
I am water really,
Know me

As you wash your hands.

PORTRAIT OF A MIDDLE-AGED MAN

The years have hemstitched his face,
Left his busy speech unchanged,
The same weasel eyes, the quick look,
All was here — though
The party-line less pronounced.

We stood, drinks in hands, and stared,
Our minds, in a double-act, shook
From the young man in khaki
To the one with a stoop who

Took great pains to show me
His life's gangrene:
The wife he had failed and fled from,
The daughter who leapt to her death,

The great book he could write but
Won't now ... the earth he had shod
And shared with a thin streak of blood:
His own labour with roses.

From
FAMILY ARRIVALS
(1981 & 1992)

WAVING

'Poor men,' my gentle mother said,
'Let's wave to them, they have no joy!'
And from the train, her frantic arm
Waved to those men in zebra stripes,
The prisoners, hacking at stones.

Some dared return that gestured hope;
A germ, a spark — swift as the train —
That blanched their black, everyday fear
With quick significance of life:
A waving woman and her child.

FAMILY ARRIVALS

There is the same excitement at their coming,
Here, where the ballet of the airport shudders;
I feel the forecast of their certain summer.

A generation past I saw the shunting
Of steam and wheels as backcloth to arrivals,
And sensed the fever in my mother's waiting.

For them the hours of travelling are the same;
Though continents and destinations change,
Their shoulders rounder and their walking slow,

They bring their love now in transparent hands.
In pain we cross a platform of a past
And see the missing ones we dare not name.

GRANDFATHER

For me
He was the unassailable giant.
The creator of bicycles and dolls,
The law of God behind his butcher's apron.

He smelt
Of sausages and fresh air,
And he grew out of his small town
As naturally as a Black Forest pine tree.

Not quite
In tune he would sing to me,
With tears in his voice and eyes,
His well-worn folk-songs and ballads.

His word
Was gospel to his family,
And his wife's large domesticity
Was ornament and shape for his great size.

No one
Dared to correct him.
For him it was right to stub his roll,
To saturate his moustache and napkin,

So when
One April Fool's Day
They barricaded his shop and house,
He, like an angry god, turned away from the living.

THE TABLECLOTH

A tablecloth,
A white, coarse linen weave,
A dead thing, so it seems.
Its threads are gently rent
In places, as in dreams,
When falling into pits
We wake in unbelief.

So frays this weft.
My father's mother made
The cloth in quiet days.
What patient thoughts she wove
Around this loom, narrow
Village ways, important
Hours underlined her shade.

Now, when I touch
This fragile web, and spread
It with our wine and bread,
And watch it slowly die,
I grieve not for its breach
But for the broken peace,
The rootlessness, our dread.

ATTIC

We stored some dusty things up there.
It smelt of mothballs and bare wood,
A spaceless jumble place to hide.
All day we crouched below the sun
Too young to feel the utter fear.
We heard them scream and beat with sticks —
Now they were near —
      a widow's world
Crashed through her glass, old limbless
Porcelain and brass, her table
Torn from her late, careful touching.
We trembled.
      Someone shouted: 'Halt,
Der Fuehrer will das Treiben nicht!'
And all was quiet.—
      Then my mother
Cooked some food, and we were waiting
For my father's earth-worn footfall
Returning from the darkening trees.

THE RED CROSS TELEGRAM

The red-cross telegram
Read when it came
Those five and twenty words;
The terror, fear,
Was there; I did not dare
To grasp the cruelty
That now I know
It did contain:
'We have to move,
Our residence will not
Remain this town,
Farewell, beloved child.'
How can I ever sing
A requiem
In silent, dark despair,
Transfiguring
Your calvary of nails
And gas and graves.

CHESS

He sits all day and plays his game of chess.
Alone — a champion of retirement.
This round is won, this last decade of sums
Shrinking his time into a silent square.

He knows he is the master of success
After those years of metal, hooks and knives,
That stiffened fingers, shrunk his bones, his neck,
Clawing his days into a spine of care.

He wears a mandarin's impassiveness.
But now — for a most concentrating move:
His eyes are sharper and his queen secure —
'Check Mate' he roars across the empty chair.

DEPORTATION

What do we know of nights in cattle-trucks,
Of fires dying on a wire fence,
Of their despair,
Or their release in fumes,

Of their suspended sentence, freezing stance,
And hunger in the ruins of their flesh,
Or of their souls,
Could they still hear the chant?

Some days the lash tears at my skin and bones.
What right have I to soak defeat in fears,
Wet with my tears
My well-fed, balanced face?

I want to lie with them in unknown graves
And bury freedom of indulgent years.
There is no judge
To hear and end their cause.

SOMETHING I HEARD TODAY

Something I heard today
Reminded me of that long corridor,
The polished silence caught behind each face —
I'd never been inside that place before.

Police — Gestapo were
Vocabularies that shared my growing pains,
Familiar yet abstract as names of squares.
But here we sat and stood in wordless queues.

Three generations waiting
In the narrow light that pressed like lockjaw
On our brains.
        My turn. I went into a
Room, beside a table that still seemed to grow,

And someone grabbed my hand
And stained my thumb and fingertips with ink,
And pressed the spiral secrets from the nerves
On paper.
        Something died then, on that desk.

Later, when walking home
Through town, I well remember how I felt:
Not the indignity — I minded most —
But that dumb theft with my, too helpless, hand.

STONE-SETTING

For thirty years
I locked your nameless graves.
I stamped on grief
When it assumed the days
And hid the dark
That slept inside my brain.

I could not speak
Of you. But you were here:
Deep, in my son's
Known eyes, in fisted streets,
On mountain's glass,
And in a valley's heat.

Like you, I felt
That river bleed through me.
Now I unbolt
Your earth, try to incise
On gravestone's bark
My words of branching peace.

I share my scars
With each young orphan's wound,
And man's blind guilt.

STRASBOURG

The air smells of childhood.
The mansard roofs
Let down their grey aprons

While tourists confuse
The naming of stones
At the foot of the Munster.

On broad, cobbled pavements
Two languages meet
In a polka of sayings

That has weathered the wars;
The markets are rich
With ripeness, the wine

Leaves its medals
On nights that grow gentle
By suede canals without scars

But still mocks the bridge
Where that old tyrant river
Holds the balance of borders.

JEWISH CEMETERY IN PRAGUE

(for Rabbi Lov, creator of the Golem)

Roots creep and coil themselves
Round skeletons, eight deep,
Inside the dust of Prague.
Trees roof the narrow space.

So, tightly packed, the generations
Keep their silence here.
The wise man and the teacher
Fold away their mysteries;

The Golem's shadow haunts
The deep, while hundreds come
To touch these witnesses, to find
Some faith with ancestors.

And underneath the Vltava
Has stretched her arms
To gather back the seeds of souls
Into a central European sea,

While stones, some leaning on each other,
And heavy with inscriptions,
Are slowly sinking every year
Towards the rooted dead.

SONG FOR A SEPTEMBER BIRTH

for Joanna

Last wheat of summer,
Sun inheritor,
This world has gleaned you
As a tiny grain,
As confirmation
Of a labour's light,
The shock of birth still
Playing round your head.

Prepared stand winter
Seasons to receive
Your breath of brightness,
And a sleep will help
The earth continue
Till your dance returns
Its greening skyward
Rhythm, year by year.

Workmate of living,
Small comrade in arms,
One battle over for you
Yet another starts,
We stare in wonder,
Bless your busy fists
And feet, your complete
Brave contingent here.

From
A LIFELONG HOUSE
(1983)

APRIL WIND

Here, under the sky's wide wheel
The wind sharpens the day's blade.

April has come with abrupt
Harshness, mocking the shy sun,

Blazing the blossom's softness
Over the shivering grasses.

Shadows are as restless as
Nervous fingers, unable

To find the day's knot and measure;
Bullfinches, in a sudden fit,

Sit and strip our apple-tree
Of buds — so much destruction

Unrolling in this low land;
An augury of rough spring

Falling on hill country, one April,
Years ago, when the breaking

Of glass stunned my grandfather's
Heart, not dead, in this wind's cry.

WILD GARLIC

And still the smell of wild garlic
    Will cling to my fingers;

It must be more stubborn than Romans
    Who brought its first flower.

We came to that wood expecting
    Familiar bluebells

And found a white weed, as spiky
    As shavings of egg-shells,

And smelt the sharpness of robust
    Italian cities.

I'd never seen it, this comma
    On Hadrian's pages,

But you could explain its obstinate
    Seed — as you always do.

TRANSMUTATIONS

The animal smell
Of the hawthorn hedge
Pulls me to the edge of the field.

It is older than
This white blossom's name
In the shrub's tight leaves, like crosses.

Shadows are deepening
In the late sun's light
Sharpening each thorn to a dark nail,

And almost with fear
I touch the full bough:
It spills ashes, blinding my shoes.

EQUATION

As a child I began
To fear the word 'Jew'.
Ears were too sensitive.
That heritage was
Almost a burden.

Then broke the years of war
In a strange country.
This time they sneered at me
'German' as blemish,
And sealed a balance.

INTO DUSK

for June

We collect fenland half-tones
On rubbery grass and earth,

Along slow lizard-skins of water
Where deliberate swans

Slide by in their kingship,
No longer flake-white.

For an uneven minute
The last cloud-marred streak of sun

Reaches its orange crescendo
Giving quick blood to our eyes

Before mist has the hungry word.
On the far side of the river a house

Still brags of solidity,
The size of a fingernail,

And turning, we see the sure
Skull-blur of the cathedral

Pulling us to cut-glass
complexities of the city.

FACES

I

After long miles of heat,
After tall fields of wheat and corn
On soil too dark with blood,
The day had flattened into August night.

And we had come to Reims:
A crust of lights in caves of stone,
The angel's island face,
His crystal smile on a staircase of saints.

II

That night they stood outside
The restaurant, their bodies bent
And stiff, moving thin hands
Like sorting lentils on a window sill.

Yes, they had faces too,
Those fingers gripping rubbish bins;
Fleshless, intent and slow
They grinned between the rags and paper bags.

MEANINGS

I

The pain has brought a brilliance to his eyes.
Something invades him, adds a foreign spark
Not known before. If pain really ennobles,

Gives a clue to years and haste, may be
He finds it now, here in this dustless ward,
In brutal hours that cleave him from us,

Take him to the start of knowledge: bewildering
To himself he probes his own existence
And beyond. — 'His threshold must be fairly low'

They say 'we are not used to seeing him
Without bounce.' A smile attacks his harnessed face —
Like wind lifting a sadly rising kite.

II

Again the man surrenders to the child
And pain is uppermost. Outside
The day surrounds the falling light
As apricots bruise on cathedral stones.

'Think positive' they say.
                                    I try to see
Beyond his feverish face, to think
Of Mozart's music and the time of spring,
I even pray in that old chant that weeps,

And envy those who live in prayer:
Who can accept. Then there are other thoughts:
Of those who suffered not in beds,
Who had to queue for death — I look

At him — the pain has eased, he smiles.
Another evening passes and the visiting
Is over. I gather clothes, and corridors,
And stairs, and he demands my gift of sleep.

III

Behind the glass he breaks the hours down
Grafting each second to a separate skin
To coat the slow monotony of days.

His patience flakes like paper from his brow
As waiting measures April clouds that spin
All seasons in a shadow game of shapes.

From streets and measurements of different sounds
We come into this ailing smell of spring,
Balancing flowers, fruit — even some love —

Yet cannot enter quite; only a mood
Invades, the stare of pain and illness clings —
Enlarging time and grief beyond the glass.

IV

Lately, death has been with me all the time.
Not as a threat, or morbid aftermath,
But like a distant relative my mother

Talked about some years ago: someone who
Will insist on intimate exchange, who
Captures every shadow that I throw.

The more I struggle, keep my distances,
The more he lurks behind each dinner guest
And waits for me to introduce him there.

So, always now, I must prepare myself
To perforate the safety-net between us,
Make him welcome, get to know him, bid him: go.

V

This travelling has the passiveness of sleep.
A 'white Maria' with sophisticated eyes
That green and shade the world outside
Where acid fields of mustard hint at light.

A toddler with embroidered boots eats endless sweets
While his expecting mother fights the terror in her eyes.
And he, whose body bears my journey's cause,
Has found a stoic's adumbration on his face.

Often these ambulances hold neutrality:
As uncommitted movements between poles,
In perforated half-light pinned to pain
While in the yellow world outside someone escapes.

VI

He walks like one afraid to step on stones.
Uncertainties drip from his fingertips
And monsters hide behind each tree, each house.

The air is alien too: as hard as flint
It penetrates his eyes and cuts through head
And lungs. They have to find a meeting place,

His body and these elements that now
Are threat and domination. Somehow, they
Must succeed. A point of recognition,

Old as Adam, waits to give him courage.
Then he can lose the luggage of his pain,
The thick security of wards, and touch

The presence of the day. But also, he
Will have to learn again to carry fear
Without the sagging of his shoulder blades.

WOMEN IN DRESS SHOPS

They come in eager to confide.
Baring their bodies,
Part of their confession,
Each sagging limb a pediment.

And from their outer wools and tweeds
That camouflage the scent
Hiding detection
Down to the intimates of flesh

They spend themselves; because at last
They're able to obtain
An ear, an interest
That will flatter them expensively.

Later, when they have left the shop,
Each tale still travels on
In darts, and hems, and pleats,
To its own hushed senility

While we, with empty echoes, take
The threads and wrap them round
Our own fragili ties
To toughen up the seams of love.

GOOD FRIDAY

This Friday, which to you
Is dark and Good,
Making a paradox
Of sin and birth,
Of blood that questions mine-
Can it explain
Our need of guilt and hope?

Yes, I have knelt on stones
And sensed some peace,
As I have knelt in woods
Blessing the roots of trees
(The nightshade standing tall).
I've heard the secrecy
Of bursting corn,
Marvelled at mineral
Below the clay
Dispersing grass for greed.

I've circled in the note
That hurts the heart,
In terror — tenderness
Of love; in words
That move beyond the day
Replacing time
Where everything is paired:

As mothers kneel
In every woman's breath,
And sons
In every man's desire.

FUGUE

There was no irony in it,
After their nightfall arrival.
She always came shadowless now.

This time she brought one in his black
Swastika uniform. They ate
As usual at the oak table.

Then, in the yellow light's comfort
The older woman's accurate
Fingers unpinned a stepping fugue.

His words cut that afterglow calm:

'I did not believe that a Jew
Could play Bach like that, I thank you.'

GHETTO

Gettare — Ghetto. In tall, stiff-necked houses,
Ring inside ring.
       Sunless under hot sun.

A foundry in Venice hammered that word,
Fisted its shape.
       Sunless under hot sun.

The anvil's drumming made metal to bone,
Flamed lead to blood.
       Sunless under hot sun.

DIALOGUE

Too fertile with felled blood,
Acres of Northern France.
Dark squares of dumb crosses
Browbeat the sun. Tall shrines
Shock flat fields, heavy with
Harvest. He remembers
That last brutal battle
Of Caen, cursing again.

Later that night, a bright
'Stube', a beer-clanking
Crowd. Holiday happy.
A muscular German
Proud of his prisoner
English, tells of his flight
Out of the hell at Caen.
Both in the same red earth.

Now they drink to friendship.
'What are you?' 'A doctor,
You?' 'Ferryman, Christian.'
'I am an English Jew.'
Blisters of sweat cover
The German's face. He lifts
His hands, halting despair.
Sober, their crosses fall.

KOL NIDREI

Father, unlock my dawn, my vows,
Fail not —
I saw the nightshade standing tall
In woods
Of yesterday, the sudden leap
And clasp
Of valleys deep and free, the pain of loss
As friend.

Back in a sky-licked land the weight
Of stones
That sink before world's night gives lies
To men;
The dead leaves of a rose are sick
With scent;
My feet are black with clay, light haunts
My hands.

They, in their shuttered ghetto swayed
With vows,
When that feared whisper crept below
Their chant
Dropping their prayer-shawl slowly
They went —
Kol Nidrei Adonai, forgive,
Repent.

GRANDMOTHER

She could walk no further
    Than the garden gate,
Her black skirt dusting hot sand;
    Where the yellow heat
Bent down to us as it spanned
      — From a sunflower's face —
Her slowing bones that belied
    Her agile eyes.

In their brightness quickened
    Eighty years of life:
The wisdom of long widowhood;
    The time of briskness;
The stride to the waterpump;
    To the bales of cloth
She had wound and unwound like
    Multi-coloured snails.

Her look hunted hardship:
    That barbed-wire gaze
That had governed her five sons
    Still ruled without words
From a filigree frame.
    And the linen she wove
With a sun-shy hand still cools
    And calms my face.

A DRAMATIST WHO WAS MY FATHER

All day, on Sundays,
He walked in the woods, alone,
Needing exhaustion.

The mushroom silence
Of trees tuned his voice,
The sudden brightness

Of meadows glazed
And bandaged his icon-wounds
Of unwritten words.

At home, old manuscripts
Yellowed and mourned in dense
Drawers of his desk;

But still new lines
That would never smell ink
Or paper breathed

Their last upright
Declensions on a stage-set
Of queues and gas,

His words, now ashes,
Bitter, perpetual powder
On my tongue.

DIASPORA

Rivers — we are —
Glass mothers,
Bearing the slow barge
With its cargo of coal
From the sea's cleft throat,
To the mountain's broad heel.
There, where the water
Knuckles its knee,
By rivalry
Of bridges,
We stayed a while,
A thousand years.

Not for us:
The constancy
Of roots, of black trees
Charcoaled in deep clay;
Nor the ochre-brown stone
Carved into the slate cloud.
But we, too, return,
Altered in movement,
In the same God 's
Drenching air;
And the same light
Haunts our hands.

THE LAST OF WINTER

Today, the last of winter,
Your letter came, telling me
How you seek the sun outside
Your house now, no longer able
To travel South, so you sit on a chair
In the street for two hours, watching,
Absorbing the yellow goodness,
And gratitude breaks from your lines.

You tell me, too, of another
Who died in his sleep having
Completed his four score and five
In a museum of simplicity,
Who had travelled through many
Languages and was able to age
With his own house and land,
And his wife's quiet tears.

So I went out to the black earth
Beaded with gulls and snow,
To the high river returning
The sky's reel, inhaling
A slow sharpening of air
Where the profile of death had been seared,
Grateful for each footstep from
The streets of winter, for a face.

MANDEL'SHTAM IN EXILE

... the happy repository of heaven
is a lifelong house that you can carry everywhere.

O.M.

Always he carried his house
Through the centre of pain
Counting the spine of his days,
Brittle in exile,

He could bleed his words on a table
In tender flames,
Or stand by the window in silence
Caressing the young hills,

He could cut the stone-air
With a soldier's song,
Breathe in alien sand
Yet his cry was water,

He could move through lies of iron
Saying the password: rust
And part the black-voiced curtains
For the sky's whisper.

THE CURE

A narrow tower, old, six hundred steps,
I took an oil-lamp, climbed and counted, prayed,
Before I reached two hundred light had failed.

I felt the dank old monster's jealous breath
Like lava on my face: no turning back —
A narrow tower, old, six hundred steps.

This was the way to Hades, desolate,
No Charon rowing me across the Styx;
Before I reached two hundred light had failed.

The sodden stone-walls held me in their fangs
Pulling the spiral rooted in my head;
A narrow tower, old, six hundred steps.

Someone inside my throat rang stony bells,
A voice as alien as a Caliban's;
Before I reached two hundred light had failed.

A sudden whiteness — triumph was ahead!
Later, descending, I sang all the way;
A narrow tower, old, six hundred steps,
Before I reached two hundred light had failed.

FRIENDS

To call you faithful would not be enough.
You came at night because the laws were wild
With hate. It could have meant a broken, rough
Diminished life for you and for your child;

It could have been your end. But when they burnt
The temples, when they rent the doors apart
That held our coffined world, when they interned
And chained the silent men and many hearts

Translated fear to death, you found the way
To us. Even before the cattle-trucks
Ordained a new stage of the cross, that day,
Your comfort marked a constancy. It brushed

All bitterness away I might have clutched
As a distorting mask. With love you judged

THREE

Not the daily dawn
Engendering noon
Until slow evening fall;

Nor the regular path
Through the forest of night
To parched valleys of sand;

But the apposite,
Cellular spark
From abrasive stones

Flaming four hands
To a random cross.
And we shall call it: Love.

From
THE SHOEMAKER'S WIFE
(1987)

ARRIVAL

When I arrived
The gate was always open,
Broad and unhinged,
The gravel underfoot
Pale apricot,
And in the house itself
The air was bright
At first. A generous
Untidiness
Past sideboards, chairs,
And tables where
So many hands had met,
Until a step, a stair, led
Unexpectedly
Into a darkness which the day
Could never sear:
Those anterooms, mysterious
Passages,
The storing corners by
A spiral stair
Held more than dust. For years
I smelt and saw them
Only in disguise.

So here was England:
By the fire-place,
The tea with scones and soda-bread,
The Irish voice
That read from Dickens, made
Him live for us;
The passion in each breath,
Her Schubert songs!
The shabby, shaking figure
Who was once an
Indian Army Colonel,
Now absorbed in roses, lawns,
And the same curry every week.

A portrait hung
Large, on her study wall:
A grandmother
From Java — beautiful
And like the rest:
A contradiction
Of this island universe.
And not one door was ever locked.

AT DOVER HARBOUR

Behind this rough sleeve of water
There lies the heart's island, set in
A harvest of stone, its work done.

Ahead, the broad hand of Europe
Opens her lined landscape, the skin
Hard and calloused with bitter blood.

And the arm heaves under grey cloth
Releasing the split signal of
The lighthouse of love with its white

Exploding star, turning always
In the black wind that calls me back
To whispering benedictions.

CHERRIES

These cherries taste of summer streets to school,
Or rather of the walk there in the heat
When stumbling over melting tar the mile
Seemed endless. Pennies in my fist, the treat

Of shiny cherries waited. The corner
Shop was rich with fruit, all ripening juices
Cased in bumper beads from black to red, more
Like a feast of pregnant marbles than these

Perishable sights. I bought and clutched them
In a coarse brown paper bag. At the first
Break, their squashy sweetness shared our game:
We stained our faces, ears, our frocks, with thirst

For them, ignoring maggots that could lurk
Inside their flesh, a white curl in the dark.

GERMANY 1933

The air was dank with fifty little girls.
Spell-bound they listened to their teacher's tale
Of one young martyr*, one who gave the name
To that new hymn. They wept for him. He burnt

An early hero into ready minds.
And then the oath — they hardly knew what for —
Of loyalty to him whose massive roar
Bludgeoned their ears. There was no choice, no sign

Of something sinister. They longed to serve,
To sing in great processions, hold a flag,
And feel secure under this pagan tag.
A slag-heap waiting for a willing herd.

'Now choose the one to lead, to march ahead,
To keep your trust, unfurl the swastika.'
The teacher urged a ballot on the class.
'The one you like the most' he archly said.

The children chose and named a jewish child.

*Horst Wessel

THE SHOEMAKER'S WIFE

She came to us walking, at night.
Our bundle of mended shoes
Hot secrets in her shopping bag.

By the door in the hall she stood
And cried. Her autumn hair
Wild from the wind.

Her red-blue eyes like
Sores in her face,
Sad postmarks

From the cobbler's shop
In the narrow old town
Where her husband hammered

And stitched his days;
Where the sign 'No Jews'
Newly pinned to the door

Pleased her sons'
Keen suspicion
That mastered all our lives.

MEMOIR

On certain days
There would appear a photograph:
A young and handsome officer,
Austro-Hungarian, on her desk.
    'The one I should have married'
She explained 'he fell in the Great War.'
And next to him herself,
A soul-struck girl with eyes of coal.

At other times
A former pupil took his place:
A Leonardo face, lost to her now
In war-anaemic Hertfordshire
Here, she worked hard at living
On the land, at keeping rabbits,
Pigs, at unforgetting.
Her hands were sick with unborn music.

ON SHUTTING THE DOOR

Often, when I leave home,
I think of you,
How you'd have shut the door
That last time
They fetched you out at dawn.

What fears would prophesy,
What intimations
Could foretell the terrors
Of those plains,
The herding into ash?

Or maybe, you looked round
As if before
A holiday, leaving
No trace of dust,
No crumbs for pests, no moths

In cupboards, carpets;
Covered the chairs,
The settee from the glare
Of light and sun,
Turned off the water, gas...

NEIGHBOURS 1942-43

So this was how they went:
With layers of clothes
Prepared for ice.
Some gems and coins
Sown into hems,
Perhaps to help escape.

You came the night before
To stem their dark.
To lay your words
On open souls
And bind with hands
A will to outlive hell.

But when your husband fell
In Warsaw's fight,
Left fatherless
Your child — quite close
To him they lost
That breath that willed my life.

TWO BOYS 1940-44

Two boys played on a farm in France.
Quite ordinary boys. 'No harm
Will touch them', so the farmer priced
His promise for a bar of gold.
He stored and fathered orphaned lives.

Before their bones had stretched full size
Their minds were strung with adult ache.
In earnest they played 'Blind Man's Buff'
Or 'Hide and Seek'. They knew the ways
Of tunnelled moles and fumbling bats.

Their growing pains had hostile names.
Their town-hands learned to crumble soil,
To master trees, to sweat with fear.
We thought them safely caged in barns.
What made him break their padlocked years?

To let the hunter grab his prey
And shunt them on an eastern train
In cattle-trucks to nameless graves
Where fathers never heard them groan:
Amen — for their dumb growing pains.

How did he plough his land and reap
With children's ghosts, their splintered nails,
How did he clean his grubby skin
From their cold questions in its cracks
And shrug away his ailing sin?

THERE

In that street it was always summer;
Hot enough to sit on slabs
Of paving stones, watch grown-ups pass,
Be recognised as my mother's daughter.

There was the tall doorway which led
Through chill darkness into the yard
Where a dung-heap blossomed
In competition with geraniums;

Where the butcher-boy sang as he scoured
A stable or laughingly lassoed
A rope of intestines above his head;
A goat's white kick sharpening the air.

An earth world so divorced
From school and town, from elegance
Partitioning the year's performance,
But warm and sweet as my aunt's yeast buns.

AUNT ELISE

My aunt Elise,
Daughter and sister of rabbis,
Was roundness incarnate.

Dripping with long-fringed shawl
And smelling of soap,
Of wax and wood,

She stood with the heat
In a low-beamed room
Of the black and white house:

The mothball wife
Pregnant with prayer
She curled her hands

And widened her eyes
Like frightened pennies:
Questioning her childlessness.

CHANT OF A RETURN VISIT

Hour after hour the day takes its toll:
I walk where I played, where I learnt the first
Singing, heard the alphabet dancing.

Tramlines still snaking through narrow streets,
Market women with expressionist stalls
Splashing their speech over pot-pourri smells.

I stand by the grass with the cited stone,
By the opposite house where the window speaks
Of the child inside and the burning night.

And behind the white wall: the drone, the drone,
Of the ancient chant that I dare not hear,
Where new faces peer over prayers that weep

Telling of other walls crumbling: 'Oh hear,
Oh Israel hear! Our God is One, is King!'
But the child cannot go where the woman stands.

She walks to the Rhine, to its clear refrain
From the time of her birth to this day that is old
With tunes of eyes, asphalt and stone.

SCHULS TARASP REVISITED

(for my father)

Dear marching hero, tracing your long strides
Along the boulders of the river Inn
Walking away the demons of your mind,
I feel their tremor on the bridge and run

When crossing to the gorge. You loved that Spa:
The elegance beside the steaming spring,
The promenading while you sipped that raw
And sulphurous drink, the afternoons that cling
To Kurhaus gardens, coffee, schmalzy dance,

Light years away from hostile marching songs.
They cushioned you, those quiet weeks, the rhythm
Reeking of Edwardian follies and their time
(And yet between two 20th century wars)
When mountains could displace that crooked cross.

No premonition then of that dark curse
That would destroy your summers, seal my loss.

FOR FRIEDRICH SANDELS
(March 14 1889-August 5 1984)

> ... 'Immerhin! Mich wird umgeben
> Gotteshimmel dort wie hier,
> Und als Totenlampen schweben
> Nachts die Sterne über mir.'
>
> Heinrich Heine, 'WO?'

I

Today I walked in his flat birth country;
The soil still sandy, the Rhine massive.
Born in that corner of the river's knee
He was rooted in a delta of vines,
Could reach out in safety for mountains and seas,
Know and teach many legends and lives.
His creed was Greece, his voice was German.

He straddled the Kaiser's field-grey years.
Then clarity purged each failed decade.
His oracle told of the blackest sights
Which no one believed, no one would fear
Until his Delphic burden proved true.

II

On the day of the burning school
He came walking towards us,
Face as grey as his flapping coat:

'Children' he said
'Our headmaster is dead.
His house in splinters,
His room full of gas.

They only smashed my records.'

III

He was forest and meadows,
River and Lieder,
Would praise the grace
Of the poem, the word.
The bright spine of language
Brought yeast to his blood.
History moved
As water's kinship
Leading us through
Odyssian journeys.
He taught us to weep
With Antigone's pleading
Where law was compassion,
Was courage and love.

IV

'Weep for his passing,
Sing for his living,
Give thanks for the seed
Of his harvest words.'

V

'Justus', his nickname, honoured him.
A celebration of his fair concern
For justice, law and discipline.

We could accept his code of decency,
Learn to respect another's private sphere
And all that forms a friend's identity.

Later, when a new country claimed his word
Of different subjects, languages and creeds,
He marched for civil rights among the crowd.

His Europe changed, became a holiday
Where peaks were climbed by cable-cars, not sweat,
And where a boy's Greek grammar made him cry.

Still anxious in his ninth decade
His letters emphasized his mind's great zest
Probing into and through each complex world.

The day the message came that he had died
I spent in making bread, in kneading dough.
His presence in this ritual close at hand.

CIRCUS FIRE

Only a bus-full
Of wire and mud,

Singed blackness
Where hair and skin

Had housed flesh,
Blood and bones.

The rhythm of beaks,
Of quick-eyed feathers

A teaspoon of cinders;
Serpentine reptiles

A chaos of cogwheels.
But unprepared

For human eyes:
In pairs, embracing,

The remnants of apes.

THE HOUR

The wire mesh of trees across the street
Tells of a garden now in winter dark,

An empty kitchen's whiteness underneath
Hangs in a basement as suspended life.

No sound creeps through this Sunday afternoon
When windows can be satisfied with light

In a surburban house. Air sleeps alone.
And somewhere now there are the frozen ones,

The old, the lovers without gestures, bled
And bored with such a day. — As quietness

Loops round and round the room, brushing at fear,
It almost prays, almost implores the desk,

The lamp, the chair, to brandish words inside
Another hour's question and retreat.

STOCKTAKING

Three score achieved, secured with pen and ink:
Prescriptions free and half fare on the train,
The pension pennies trickle from the bank.

Reductions now at concerts make you blink
And study price-lists with new eyes again.
Three score achieved, secured with pen and ink.

What else is cheaper? Neither food nor drink
But haircuts, inch by inch the same refrain:
The pension pennies trickle from the bank.

Where up to now you spurned the truth and sank
Years that appeared too many and a stain:
Three score achieved, secured with pen and ink.

True, waistlines will expand and chests will sink
All despite eating fibres, wholefood grain.
The pension pennies trickle from the bank.

And what of passions, hope, the heartbeat lump
Thudding in throat and voice? All still remain.
Three score achieved, secured with pen and ink.
The pension pennies trickle from the bank.

USELESS

While mothers wail, the children starve and die,
The wheat lies useless on the surplus hill
Because there is no gold in their young cry.

Now is the time of beet-smoke in the sky
And blanket-heavy hangs that malted smell
While mothers wail, the children starve and die.

We coddle cats and dogs and wonder why
Some lie spreadeagled in the road, quite still,
Because there is no gold in their young cry.

To save our men from heart disease we try
To follow doctors' anti-butter drill
While mothers wail, the children starve and die.

The cattle vanish as the milk runs dry;
Our dustbins reek with wasted food and spill;
There is no gold in those young children's cry.

The four winds gather substance for each lie,
The spokesmen eat their words against their will
While mothers wail, the children starve and die
Because there is no gold in their young cry.

NEW YEAR'S EVE

We hardly noticed that old knotty tramp
Wolfing his food (a place near Leicester Square)

Until there crossed a steel of voices, rush
Of shoes: 'Two pounds you owe us, you'll not go

Before you've paid!' He rumbled broken words,
Half sentences, tried running to the door

But fists came clamping down to trap him, push
Him to the basement stairs; one final kick,

Threat of police, was all we heard. Cowards,
We were, who sipped the year's last cup of tea

In silent fellow-travellership when faced
With hunger, cruelty, our undone deeds.

MATTMARK, Switzerland

The air, thin tissue razored white,
Wraps up this dam, this milky green
That curls from shore to shore. Birds cut

Their angles to the rocks and each
Small plant must prove its tough resilience
To the wind. The sun is bleaching

Grass like hair. Hard, out of stone, like
Diamonds, men's faces stare at us
Their early deaths: all makers

Of this place. False flowers fringe their names.
The waters, peerless, foam and shout
Their glacier song. The switch of power waits.

QUINCES

One year
The quinces hung like lanterns
From the tree,
Their amber sweetness harvesting
A light
That glows and trembles through
The jars;
The jelly set in slithering
Rounds of glass
Hoarding the taste of autumn's
Heavy gold,
Melting the ice of winter
From our tongues.

NOVEMBER

After the words the wind
Crashes round the house
Fisting the bricks,

The eaves ache under the roof
Crying out to the trees
In their cousinship,

The night arrives in a dark sheet
Calling the day's tumult
To a vesper of sleep

In this menopause of the year,
This auburn change of tired leaves
When light turns inward.

WORDS

Words tell me to iron out seconds,
To pepper the precis of years.

In one small cobweb they touch
Fragrance and method of thought.

Call it a wound or a serpent's voice
Bleeding sounds at the nerves' barricade,

The sister spider of evening
Waiting under the day's bandage.

From
EARTHQUAKE and other poems
(1994)

POWER CUT

Suddenly the television died
That late Sunday afternoon
When dusk threatened into dark:

Unused to shadowless silence
I hunt for candles
Stowed away for years

In some understair hold;
Distant 'safe rooms'
Plugged against poison.

I bleed white wax into saucers
On the kitchen table,
Huddle by the gas oven's lit throat

And read flickering words
Of poems that leap up
In triumph over this muteness.

From our cavern I watch
How blackness intensifies
Punctured by flashlights of cars

As we slide deeper into night
With its blur and footsteps,
Take comfort in uncertainty

Of the almost limbo
Where loss congregates
On the far side of sleep

Until, in an explosion of light
Noises intrude and demand
The deep-freeze whines again.

EARTHQUAKE

'Please save my brother, he's still there' he said
Clutching his pen, wearing his pin-stripe suit
Though dust and mortar stiffened him to lead.

The rubble falling round him and his head
Dizzy and bleeding. 'I'm an accountant,
 Please save my brother, he's still there' he said.

It took six seconds for the earth to shed
Her mother image and destroy its root
When dust and mortar stiffened him to lead.

Too few can crawl to safety from their bed,
Escape the knock at dawn, the vicious boot.
'Please save my brother, he's still there' he said.

Pompeii choked. No time for wine and bread.
Vesuvius boiled and strangled every street.
The dust and mortar stiffened him to lead.

We walk away from craters, feel instead
Some kind of grief for one whose world is mute.
'Please save my brother, he's still there' he said
Though dust and mortar stiffened him to lead.

DEAD RHINE

That river cannot weep,
Poison has starched his eyes
To a witches' frost of sleep.

Where once, a child, I slipped
Into his soft green silk
And loved the slimy steps

That led me down, now stand
The mourners coffin-deep
Watching the dry-eyed land

Lament a dark disease
That from some human hands
Flung devils to the trees,

To waters and their beasts.
Oh plunge your fists through fears
And find a ring that keeps

Tenure and faith with tears.

*Note: people were mourning in this way when toxic waste
poisoned the river.*

A NEW SUBJECT

'Today we start a subject that is new
To everyone. As your new master now
I've come to tell you something of those true
Great ancestors we have. You must be proud,

You boys, our fatherland, our new decade,
Is nurtured by a giant race: red-blond,
Eyes blue, a strong physique and unafraid.
The finest ethnic heritage is ours.

Let's see the type of man we used to be —
Yes you — just there — behind that darkish head,
You in the seventh row — get up, come here!
What is your name? Ah, Heinz, ah, very good.

Now face the class. You see in this blond boy
The perfect specimen of purest race;
His bones are powerful, his hair is fair,
His eyes are blue set in an eager face.

No shameful mixture in his blood or breed.
This is your future now, our Germany!
You grin — you laugh — you too — I'll have no cheek
From anyone! What is the matter, speak?'

'Please Sir, it makes no sense, it's true, you see
Heinz is a Jew.'

CISSIE

Her name was Cissie
And she mangled sheets,
Her hair was peroxide yellow;
She crooned about love
With a smoker's cough
While the sweat slipped down her belly.
She could tell a tale
Full of sex and ale
As the mangle wheeled her story,
And her laughter roared
As her bosom soared
When she slapped the sheets to glory.
In a war-time pub
Some G.I. pick-up
Cheered the Monday morning queues,
But below her pride
Of the good-time night
Were a lonely woman's blues.
For once in a while
A black eye would smile
From her puffy face full of sweat;
And we knew it meant
Her old man had spent
The infrequent night in her bed.
So she rolled and roared
As she laughed and whored
Till one day she clocked-in no more:
No G.I. or mate
Kept her out so late —
But a Buzz-bomb had struck her door.

CENTRAL CEMETERY, VIENNA

'Gate four' you asked,
The woman flinched
But then pointed the way.

And so we entered
Through the Jewish Gate
To find the silent density

Of graves. The one
You looked for, near
Some fallen stones, still

Upright, barely
Readable and overgrown.
'Johanna Spinka 1852-1935'.

The grandmother,
Agile and small. A boy,
You filled her false-teeth cup

With onion rings.
You pinched the cakes
She baked before she died.

A good age then,
Not like that evil time
When plots stayed empty here.

Now only names
Commemorate
These absences where trees

Throw shadows
Over tortured script,
Over the patient grass.

POST-WAR I

Time was, when for the price of 1/6
We'd go to the pictures, saw the B-one first,
Trailer, the news, and then the main big fix;
My hanky at the ready for a burst
Of damp emotion. Three hours at least
Of therapeutic wallow kept us sane
In that post-war austerity, a boost,
After a day of tooling the machine
For you, or sweating at a laundry
Calender, for me, with aching back
And legs. This was our weekly luxury.
Then we'd walk home to our two rooms; with luck
There was a shilling for the gas. The loo,
The bath, were shared, the dripping geyser too.

POST-WAR II

Then I'd rush home at night and look for mail
From Europe, via the Red Cross, maybe,
To say my parents had been traced, though frail
And ill but still alive ... a dream for me

And many others. A sterile make-belief
That led to nightmares, split my mind. The days
Were filled with slogging work. I buried grief,
Hunted for rations, joined banana queues.

Now looking back from years they never reached
I wonder who she was, this person 'I'
Who rushed up the bare stair-boards that we shared

With other tenants in the house. I try
Pursuing her into our two-room flat
And will not find that letter on the mat.

POST-WAR V

Your letter, searching for me, crossed with mine
Searching for you. My 'Wahlverwandtschaft' older
Sister in enemy country. Not one sign
Of bitterness. Knowing of bombs and fire

Where we used to play and fearing for your
Life so many times, to see your writing
On the envelope crossed grief with joy. For
Now you told me how you fled still carting

Those mementos that my mother brought at dawn,
Her curfew visits, how you saved your child,
Your mother too. But war had meant destruction
Of our town, and worst: had felled your husband.

In those first letters we nailed down our tales
Of you as widow, I as orphan, balanced scales.

POST-WAR VI

In France there was some heirloom jewellery,
Smuggled and hidden in the Nazi years,
Now found again and mostly ownerless.
It crouched inside my palm as family

Survivor. I recognised the bracelet
And the ring, Victorian brooches set in
Filigree with weeping rubies. Secret
Histories escaping in a tin

From gas and ash, divorced from neck and arm,
The warmth that cradled them in Kaiser's time
Or later in the 20s decadence.
Now, in the island's twilight, life or chance

On certain days will bring these items out
To give them air, to mourn, to celebrate.

COCOON

She says she can't remember anything
Of people, language, town; not even school
Where we were classmates. Her smile is frail
And hides behind her husband's hypnotising

Quietness. 'A Suffolk man' he beams,
And squares his tweedy frame against some
Unseen advocates who might still claim
An inch of her. She is content, it seems,

To lose her early childhood; he is near.
Protector or destroyer, it's his war.
He underwrites her willed amnesia,
Helps her to stifle terror, exile, fear.

She is cocooned, safe as an English wife,
Never to split that shell and crawl through love.

CONTACT

I'll keep this green cone
With the faint cedar scent,
A candle you plucked
From the tree as I left.

The resin wept down
Its pineapple curve
And sealed our hands
With the glue of its sap.

Now lustre still clings
To the side that I touch,
Feel the soft liquid purge
Our spiral of years.

HOMESICK

Still the same search for home.
Not a return,
Nor familiarity,
But the once-known
Threshold of otherness.

Years wipe away
Your fingermarks. Your chair
Is too clean; too
Much light waits in this room;
These curtains fall

Together pointlessly.
Other voices
Carpet the stairs, picture
A wall, a nail
Curls against their colours,

Breaks inside me.
I must look for a place
Without echoes:
Hope will breed in a bed
Of hopelessness.

CELEBRATION

To celebrate the house
They built the roof

And with the roof's completion
Came the child

And in her hands she held
The sapling tree

The tree with coloured ribbons
In the wind

And in the wind she moved
With careful steps

Along the planks
That led up to the height

The gabled height
Where stood the cheering men

And cheers were guiding her
From all around

Till she had brought it safely
To the peak

And on the peak they fixed
The ribboned tree

And baptised it with brandy
Glass by glass

To celebrate the roof
The house... the child...

IMMIGRANTS

The wolves are coming back to Germany.
Across the Polish border
Barricades are down:
The wolves slink into forests in the dark

And bring a darker Russia in their veins.
They sniff out ancient fairy tales
Trading in omens, hunger, fear,
Looking for hidden spaces under rocks.

At night they cluster by the edge of woods
In families of threes and fours,
Howling their wail of loneliness
Over the Eastern villages and plains.

LABURNUM

(Goldregen)

Laburnum,
'Golden rain',
Housed in the many gardens
I have known,
Brother of
Lilac,
Spill yellow softness
On my lawn, bring
Down and spread
Brightness
Of sun,
The ever friendship
Of each spring.

TRAIN JOURNEY TO ELY

It seems as if the tall, expressive grasses
                had a say
In this calm plain. This landscape hides its drama,
                hardly moves
From my slow train, yet dominates the sky
                or else there is
A marriage with the obdurate horizon
                where the mist
Performs its rite. The corn is still unharvested,
                it shines almost
To spite the clouds; and as we draw into the red-
                brick station
The engine drums the sound of afternoon.
                Yet underneath
The waters move; a secrecy; the endless
                reservoir
That's camouflaged with soil and grass and grain
                and has a pact
With skies. And nothing burns now, as on other
                days, when sun
Intensifies all that the earth has yielded
                and its pain.

FOR COLETTE

Through her
I take possession
Of that long, hard gaze
To know
The scarlet pulse in men,
In plants, in animals,
To tell
The charm and misery
Of us: in love with love,
To hear
In summer's alphabet
The earth-voice of a mother
To melt
The yeast of memories,
Touch with my palm, my tongue,
My shin
Each unmet thought and taste,
Inhabit houses, new
At first,
Inherit libraries
Alive with dust and smell,
Declare
The movement of each limb
As pleasure's miracle.

From
THE DESECRATION OF TREES
(1994)

OXFORD, 1940s

Then I was "Mother's Help--Lady's Companion",
A teen-age girl in love with fantasies
Walking the wartime Oxford streets and lanes.

The colleges were locked facades to me
Quite out of bounds with military use
But still regarded with romantic awe

As territories one day to he explored
By one who'd shed the enemy alien skin.
Meanwhile there were the books-some treasured

Second-hand, picked up at Blackwell's for a song.
An early Schnitzler with the spine in shreds
And hinted sex in dashes worming through

To savour secretly. Before permissiveness.
Long, lonely afternoons up Shotover,
The hill that took me past an empty church

I sometimes entered, praying in my search
For something new and weatherproof
But never found. Years looking for a clue.

A cleric gave a lecture, gaunt, severe,
On faith, a Puritan of sorts, a Scot
Who sent me down a draughty corridor

A mile or two. Not very far. 'Macbeth'
Came to the theatre and filled my head,
My bones and bloodstream ever since, the breath

Of witches stoking up my words. A flame
As permanent as air. And British
Restaurants would earn their wholesome name

With calories that lined my ribs. U.S.
Canteens were treasure troves that sometimes
Spilled their gems. And war was somewhere else.

COFFEE GRINDING

Grinding the coffee in my moulinex
The beans explode their old aroma here.
It clears the ashes out of sleep.

My mind returns to kitchens where I played:
I see our maid, broad on a stool, machine
Placed firmly between thighs:

She wheels the scent with comfortable arms
And sings of love in tune to grating knives.
A reassurance grinds.

I am reminded of another scene:
There, in the synagogue my mother stands
All day to fast and pray;

To keep her from a faintness now I bring
Some coffee finely ground, wafting a strength
Into her silent fears.

LENA, OUR MAID

She anchored all my needs
In her solidity,
A cross pleat on her brow.

Between her household chores
She'd rush with me to school,
Her rough hands square with love.

Devout, she made me kneel
On crowded pavement slabs
To watch the bishop pass

Under his baldachin
Intoning Latin chant,
The incense cloud above.

At the stone kitchen sink,
Her yeasty body's shrine,
She'd stand and strip-wash clean,

Then outings into town,
To dark room secrecy
Where she collected hope

From a clairvoyant's words
Behind a curtain fall,
Her love-life's counterpoint.

A butcher boy appeared
And many nights they sighed
On mother's lounge settee

While I pretended sleep
Two doors away. She got
Her man and left. I cried.

Her home two basement rooms
Where she would lie in wait
With plates of chips, the food

I loved, spoiling my lunch.
But still I hear her screams
Up in my room, two floors

Above her flat, when she
Gave birth to her huge son
Her second child, she said.

THE NON-EMIGRANT

(my father in Nazi Germany)

He left the application forms
Hidden inside his desk and missed
His quota for the U.S.A.

He thought he'd stay and wait and stare
The madness out. It could not last.
He would not emigrate, not lose

His home, his language and his ground.
Beside his armchair sat a pile
Of books; the smoke from his cigar

Fenced comfort with a yellow screen.
His daily walk was all he'd need,
He thought. Abroad was where he'd been.

'WIENER BLUT'

I can still hear it,
The thin waltz on the hand-wound
Gramophone in the long, baroque ball-room,
The glittering horse-shoe table
Shrouded in white,

The bride and bridegroom
Pinned to the centre like jewels
Surrounded by clusters of uncles and aunts,
A tall cousin putting on records
With a distracting grin,

And all eyes on me
In a pink tulle ballet dress
Dancing to the music and getting lost
On the geometry of the Persian carpet
When 'Wiener Blut'

Decreed its own rhythm
And I was crisscrossing another
The inevitable round of the waltz eluding
My well-rehearsed steps
To my nightmare shame

PUBERTY

The Rhineland heat hung heavy in the street.
Across the road with windows open wide
The opera singer practised his great roles.

Framed in his room's own shadow distanced him,
His naked torso white as I, half-grown,
Watched him in safety from my recessed dark.

One day he fixed my eyes with his, brought voice
And hands together in a plea, unnerved
Me with his begging aria of love.

And when he motioned me to strip as well
I stepped back terrified in secret shock,
Excited and yet unable to leave.

I told no one. We never spoke. He'd haunt
All summer. When I saw him laugh with women
In the street I'd look away and flee.

AT BURGHLEY HOUSE

We walk here
Where each tree and shrub
Is a planned cypher
In Capability Brown's charter;
Where Englishness
And Tudor stone surround us
And pale sun whitens
Our footprints in the grass.
Your questions
Curl with American vowels
As they should after all those years
Since we walked along the Rhine
On a November day
Bright with dread and ashes
When flames had taken
Our holiest places.
Overnight
We had learnt the language
Of terror, but still could walk
Carelessly, as children will,
By that river that shone.

BILINGUAL

When you speak German
The Rhineland opens its watery gates,
Lets in strong currents of thought.
Sentences sit on shores teeming
With certainties. You cross bridges
To travel many lifetimes
Of a captive's continent.

When you speak English
The hesitant earth softens your vowels.
The sea-never far away-explores
Your words with liquid memory.
You are an apprentice again and skill
Is belief you can't quite master
In your adoptive island.

Myself, I'm unsure
In both languages. One, with mothering
Genes, at once close and foreign
After much unuse. Near in poetry.
The other, a constant love affair
Still unfulfilled, a warm
Shoulder to touch.

SECOND THOUGHTS

The day
I sold some family silver
At first I felt no regret;
But then
The gaps in drawers, cupboards,
Stared back with pity and awe.
There began
The lost clutter and dance
Of salvers, bowls, spoons.
I knew it
As a kind of homesickness,
That permanent claw in the blood,
But also
As freedom from possessions,
As pleasure at parting
From things
That told and heavied the heart
With a tyrant's mirror.

BARRICADES

She is wailing in the archaic
German of her childhood
Across continents of cinders
Unthought of by doctors and nurses.

In her long-ago house
She sends us down to the cellar
Through a coal-dark door
To fetch a bottle of lemonade.

She is waiting with certainty
For her dead husband's arrival
But weeps because 'too many
Stones on the path-
       he can't cross the stones.'

Her room is my prison.
My shame is my fear
Of her plundered world
I refuse to enter.

THE DESECRATION OF TREES

(in appreciation of Peter Handke's 'ACROSS')

Someone, now well past middle-age, white-haired,
Has painted swastikas on trees. So says
The poet-writer in his book. Fiction and
Fact, maybe, though it has followed me for days

And the spontaneous murder it provoked.
What better signature of brain-washed, sick
Disciples still alive and star-struck
By that false elixir of a decade?

I look about me, see the tendrils flare,
That crooked emblem bore through brain and sleep.
The scapegoat has two thousand lives. We weep,
We try to tie a knot in time, prepare

To praise and tell our children's children of
The constant Good-a mushroom crime of love.

THE GREEN PLEASURE

There is this green pleasure
Of shelling the first peas-
The gentle thumb-press
At the top till they split open
Revealing those small pearls
Sweet and crisp for quick cooking.

Each summer I look forward
To their lips parting
With a mild pop, air escaping
From the still young pods
And watch the pot filling
With each green promise.

BLACK FOREST SONNET

II

The dark grit of wild bilberries grates
In my mouth, picked where moss and grasses stand
Thick like shampooed heads of hair, in pleats
Among tree trunks. Some firs dead with acid

Rain. But forest still saga-deep, a pulpit
For myths and histories. A sudden stone
And cross tell of a man' s murder, his throat
Cut in 1810 for eleven Gulden.

Today we walk in summer air as mild
As butter. Foxgloves high between heather
And raspberries sweeter than remembered.
A red squirrel shoots up a tree and here,

A surprise lizard dead, or pretend dead
On the path, stretched flat and grey as old lead.

A SHORT DIRGE FOR SONIA

When I was pregnant
I read the Russians,

And if you were female
I'd call you Sonia:

Raskolnikov's girl
Who was loyal and cheap,

A prostitute saint.
She knelt in my dreams.

But I had a son
And could never test

Or pursue that allusion
In furthest Siberia

To find my own daughter.

TWO WOMEN IN ROUEN

Some towns have corners that cry out the names
Of ghosts, and so in Rouen where two women
Followed me: that girl holding her sword is
Everywhere, her voices whispering high
And low, in market halls, in gabled streets,
In squares of stone that shine flamboyant
With success and age, and in that final
Newness of one church: a ship embedded
With its roof aflame spiking the sky
In metal scales of armour. And where
The half-moon pews of polished wood still
Hear her judgment, under the rounded vault
And sunlit side of coloured glass, she sings-
Her stake outside a tall, demanding cross.

Another, much more quiet and subdued
Although her woman's passion fills the streets
Where she had travelled in a coach or walks
In ecstasy and grief; where with her anxious
Eyes she tries to lunge at love inside
A dark cathedral's nave, in dusty
Small hotels by harbour walls until
Her final loneliness turns to despair.
As real and tragic as that other one
She feeds on flames of her too human needs.

RESEARCH IN CROWLAND AND PEAKIRK

(for Shirley Toulson)

The fen-light bleached the day
As we approached the abbey's
Site, watched Guthlac's stone
Become a sun-licked apricot.

And later, in the nun's large smile,
You found the confirmation
That you need, to speak of Pega's
Journey through the fens.

There we unlocked the church
And saw the stone, grey and too
Ordinary, it seemed, to hold
That sister's heart returned from Rome.

Two fenland villages affirmed
And equalled silence on that day
With whole devotion centuries ago,
Two island witnesses.

DISUSED RAILWAY LINE

Rusting and bereaved
Of the weight of wheels
The celibate line
Ladders the horizon.

Crows black-button
The grass at intervals
Depressing frost
That has sugared its blades.

We follow this flat
Staircase, aware
Of dead journeys
To destinations

Crumbling with unuse.
We negotiate gaps
In a museum of steam
Painting the sky white

As wildflowers recover
Hesitant faces
In sooty soil
Remembering their roots.

NEW POEMS (1997)

THULE

'And I have been to Thule! It has come true —
The journey and the danger of the world,
All that there is
To bear and to enjoy, endure and do —'
Louis Simpson
(My Father in the Night Commanding No)

He says he's been to Thule in the North,
That island of the poets where they seek
The ultimate.

Where the astronomer* met moon and tides
As he was sailing from his Southern sea
North, ever North.

Imagine Thule, the coldest waters break
Against its shores, remotest winds attack
The low-slung villages.

There once a king had drained his golden cup,
Then flung it to the waves and died for love
Of her whose gift it was.

Could we console our sorrows by those rocks?
Diminish ancient burdens in our blood,
Let legends live in sand?

Pytheas

ANDROGYNOUS

Long ago
There was the man in the moon.
The cold-eyed guard
Over my childhood.
He watched my nights chillingly.

Now he's turned female.
Benevolence in liquid white.
A veiled eye of knowledge
In a veteran sky,
Elusive in a cloud of history.

JUDAS

Because I loved him most
Mine was the hardest task.

He knew it; paved the way
For my betraying

And placed the cruel words
Into my mouth.

I was the instrument
Of his fulfilment:

Without my kiss
No road to calvary,

Without my cross
No risen Christ.

110

CASUALTY

My little cousin died in USA.
A stroke, they wrote.

And I remember him
Appearing on our doorstep, 1944,

In uniform, his useless arm
Still in a sling.

A Normandy survivor —
Casualty, a mother's boy

Who grew up on that beach
Compulsively.

His curly grin a sign
Of one who floats through war,

A bright facade,
A hero's barricade

He'd hamster all his days
Hiding his wounded side.

We fussed about him,
Wrapped him in a garden chair.

He slept his punctured sleep
Until he and his nightmare died.

THE GURU OF GROCERIES

In my grandfather's town,
In a corner shop,
The smell of spices bounced from the walls,

The goods in a jumble
Of tubs and jars
From fresh Sauerkraut to a mêlée of sweets.

We would skip all the way
To be greeted there
By a soft young man in a kosher-white coat:

The guru of groceries;
He ruled his domain
With his silhouette mother in a velvet back room.

Many children from school
Dropped in on their way
For a bag of sweets, a chat and a smile,

Till one day he had gone;
The shutters were down,
The place was a dead as a drowned house.

Only trickling whispers
Explained with much grief
His forbidden love, his fragile sin

With a girl, not a Jew,
Who had stayed too long.
And we never ever saw him again.

note: any relationship between Jews and Gentiles
was prohibited in Nazi Germany

VIEW FROM THOMAS MANN'S
MAGIC MOUNTAIN, Davos

I

Look down with the eyes of the ironic German
And see the century's chaotic dance:
The valley crawling with cars and houses
Where meadows had cushioned the flanks of mountains,
Where the dead were bobsleighed down in darkness
Not to disturb the Zauberberg's tenants.

II

We saw the silent sister stalk the corridors.
The glass-door banged into the dining room,
Her hand went up to heavy braids of hair
That coiled his feverish blood to ecstasy.
The talk, the laughter, the intrigues,
The air was filled with them above
The uncommitted snow,
The changing faces of the other world.

III

And though we're no longer spitting blood
Or argue with passion about knotty problems,
We climb as high as our hearts will allow
And puff with achievement on stony summits
Where air is still clean and dry and healing,
Where capsules deposit high-heeled women
To admire the view and flop into deck-chairs
Usurping the tales of those magic mountains.

ERNST LUDWIG KIRCHNER IN DAVOS, 1920-1938

Not as an outcast
He came at first
But as a constant convalescent.

He settled at the edge
Of a quiet-green valley
Rounded by a waterfall

Where his feverish knife
Carved spiky woodcuts
Of stones, trees and peasants.

His carnival brush
Returned a landscape
To fearless adventures.

The harshness subdued.
Women's faces like lanterns
Under black hats,

Their bodies starched
They stand in threes
In a spring meadow.

His colours are new:
Lightning skies pierced
By sharp-ribbed mountains,

The village a refuge,
Bright with dancing houses
And never-ending steeples;

The shooting bodies
Of girls riding in rhythms
To ascending clearness,

Yet his own earth stays hostile.
His exit as outcast:
His last determined statement.

*E.L.Kirchner's art was prohibited as 'degenerate' in Nazi
Germany. He committed suicide in 1938.*

FLAMES

She dropped her duster, shouted: "Zeppelin",
We all rushed out onto the terrace, looking up
At that fat silver fish cruising the sky.
A swimming miracle, it seemed, until
The wrong gas flamed it to a fiery lie.

Years later, in the war, you grabbed binoculars,
Jumped on the garage roof to get a view
Of that queer, manless plane lit by the sun
Above us, flames shooting from its tail
Until the droning stopped — our first V1.

We learnt to eat, to dance, to sleep with them,
Those demon flying bombs. But every time
That slash of silence blunted breath, a sigh
Of dread, quite sick with guilt we'd pray for them
To pass — and someone else would have to die.

A BRIEF WALK

i.m. Martin Howe BA AMA, 1950-1994
Curator of Peterborough Museum

He was buried on a bright October day,
The leaves put on their yellow shrouds.

His car wept early mist waiting
For his key. His five-year wife

Still clung to the fresh sound of his voice,
The electric tread of his feet.

The world knew him as a miner fetching
Nuggets of gold from quotidian earth,

As explorer of many horizons
Below and beyond the sun,

Catching and refracting light
For all to warm and colour their days.

His joy never stilled at the newness of words,
In the quick laughter he shared out.

His name will live in each life he touched,
In rooms that exhale his breath,

In stoncs that remember his language,
On the brief walk he could take among us.

FOR KATHLEEN RAINE

When bitterness wrung
Its most useless dross
Through my veins, her voice
Blessed the river's glass.

Her landscape is birth;
The sureness of grass,
The flow to the sea
From the child's mirror.

And through the late pulse
Of the train, that sound
Bled to the dark t own,
To the aloes of love.

GOYA: STILL LIFE WITH GOLDEN BREAM

These fish have been shocked into death.
Their wide-open eyes accuse.

Like thick scaly fingers
Stacked across each other

They glitter in moonlight
By the edge of the sea,

Their mouths have closed
On war sadness,

A heap of helplessness
In silver stillness,

A long way
From the frying pan.

ANECDOTE 1920s, Rhineland

"There wasn't much to eat then"
So she said,
"But space enough, you knew our flat,
Nine rooms,
The Rhine view from the balcony,
And comfortably set.
So after armistice they
Billeted
French officers with us. They whored
And spat
And lived it up, and they brought fleas —
All in my silk salon.
The maids were always pregnant,
Still, that's that. —
One was refined. He sat and talked
And smoked
Long after meals were over. Well,
You know your father's tact,
He would not hurt a fly. All
Sensitive
Benevolence, all justice, law,
Forget,
Forgive old enmities. Don't step
On any Frenchman's toes.
But on that afternoon, that
Officer
Began accusing us — as Bôches —
Of war
Atrocities. In Belgium too!
Your father sat on coal,
How I could sense his fever!
Silently
He rose and only spoke three words:
'Et les Vôtres?'
God, I was terrified. He might
Have gone to jail for that!"

IN THE STABLE HAY

Knock-kneed, alone,
The new-born calf
Stood in the stable hay.

The man approached,
Stooped over it
One arm laid round its neck,

Fed it some milk
Tilting a baby's bottle
Into sucking lips.

Then patted
The blond pelt
With scarlet hands

And wiped them clean
Along his hips
On his white overall.

He walked away.
I watched this scene
With curiosity,

A town-child's eyes
Not seeing then
He had usurped

The territory
Of mother cow.
That calf would never know

The steam of nostrils
On its side,
The rub of udders

Spilling milk,
The belly earthed
In green security.

WARSAW VIGIL 1940s

A mass in Latin,
The incense cloud
Fills the great vault
Where black-shawled women,
Knotty men
Submerge and kneel
In a shadow sea.

Among them soldiers
With black swastikas,
The enemy in prayer
Unaware of us,
The hidden Jews.
A handful only
Outside Ghetto walls.

We dare not meet
Each others' eyes
But came today
On Jom Kippur
To fast and pray
And to repent
In this safe silence.

We stay behind
As spirits almost
In the empty church,
Are camouflaged till night
As worshippers
With only Jewish Jesus
And his mother, watching.

Our thoughts are fears
For our missing ones,
Our burnt-out synagogues,
Our ruined homes.

Sometimes we move about
But do not speak.
We keep our vigil

Only venture out
As written in the law:
With the first star.

EX-COMRADES

Cold, and in poverty,
They are the old,
The disillusioned ones,
Who congregate
In cemeteries
Round unmarked graves
Where, rumour has it,
Old dictators lie
With wives and retinue.

There is no hope, they say,
For future years,
Their creed and dogma gone,
Their fought-for certainties,
Their life's work ridiculed.
Weary and hungry now
They wait to die,
Unschooled for new society
That's older than they are.

A GLASS OF WATER

Stands there, in front of you
While you turn the pages,
You look up and see through

That clearness into their
Hearsay world, the heat,
The stench, you could not share

In Poland's cattle-trucks.
The old imaginings:
Hands that beseech and pluck

At air for charity
From somewhere, water most
Of all. Your lips are dry.

You reach out for the glass
But falter, cannot drink.
A feeble gesture, this,

No help to them to let
Your thirst be paramount.
And still you cannot lift

That water to your mouth.
This afternoon you sip
Saliva, feed on breath,

Know the necessity
Of useless obsequies
In solidarity

With shadows that will stay
Beyond this glass of water's
Living chemistry.

VERSIONS

IN THE FLAT LAND

(after Rainer Maria Rilke)

In the flat land there was this waiting
for one sole guest who never came;
still anxious was the garden's asking
before its smile grew slowly lame.

And in the lazy marsh the evening
impoverishes the tree-lined road;
the apples on the branch are clinging
to fear and ache with each new wind.

From A LIFELONG HOUSE

THE BEGGARS

(after Rainer Maria Rilke)

You didn't know what that heap
consisted of. A stranger found
beggars in it. They sell
the hollow of their hand.

They show the traveller
their mouth full of muck,
and he may (he can afford to)
see how their leprosy devours them.

His foreign face dissolves
in their curdling eyes;
and they delight in his seduction
and when he speaks they spit.

From A LIFELONG HOUSE

WILL-O'-THE-WISPS

(after Rainer Maria Rilke)

We commune in old established ways
with the lights in the fen.
They seem like great-aunts to me ... and then
I discover between us

more and more that family trait
no power can suppress:
this swing, this leap, this jerk, this flight,
others try it without success.

I too am there where the roads will end
in marsh-grass many have shunned,
and often I've seen myself snuffed out
under the eyelid's hand.

From THE SHOEMAKER'S WIFE

BOTH

(after Hugo von Hofmannsthal)

She held the chalice in her hand
Her chin and mouth echoed its rim —
So light and certain was her step
She did not spill a single drop.

So light and steady was his hand
As he was riding his young horse
And with an easy gesture forced
It to a halt and, trembling, stand.

But when he should have, from her hand,
Taken the chalice, light and round,
Its weight for both was much too great
Because they both were shaking so
That not one hand the other found
And dark-red wine rolled on the ground.

From THE SHOEMAKER'S WIFE

THE DEATH OF MOSES

(after Rainer Maria Rilke)

No one, only the dark fallen angel
wanted it; took weapons, entered the death
of the assigned. But again and again
he crashed backwards, upwards,
cried to the heavens: I cannot!

Because calmly, through the brow's thicket,
Moses had perceived him and carried on writing:
words of blessing and the unending name.
And his eye remained pure to the ground of strength.

Then the Lord, tearing with him half the skies,
surged down and made up the mountain bed himself;
bedded the old man. From the ordered dwelling
he called for the soul; she arose! and told of
much that was shared, an infinite friendship.

But in the end it was enough for her. She, made whole,
admitted it should be enough. So the old God
bowed his old face slowly towards the old man.
Took him from his old age with a kiss
into his own, older one. And with hands of creation
he covered the mountain. So that there should be only
the one, re-created, among the mountains of the earth,
unknown to mankind.

From EARTHQUAKE AND OTHER POEMS

LOTUS FLOWER

(after Heinrich Heine)

(for Mouche)

Truly, we are both making
A very curious pair,
The beloved weak on her legs,
The lover lame in her care.

She is a kitten that's ailing
And he a dog that is sick;
I think both their heads are playing
A most unhealthy trick.

She would be a lotus flower,
So the darling fancies her scene;
Yet he, the pale, poor fellow,
Imagines himself as the moon.

In moonlight the lotus flower
Unlocks her little throat,
But instead of the pollen of life
A poem her only reward.

From THE DESECRATION OF TREES